Never Quit:

A 5 Week Small Group Bible Study on the Power of Prayer

By Mark Ballenger

And he told them a parable to the effect that they ought always to pray and not lose heart.

-Luke 18:1

Table of Contents

Week 1: Believe God to Not Lose Heart

And he told them a parable to the effect that they ought always to pray and not lose heart. – Luke 18:1

Life makes you want to lose heart.

Now that's a good way to start a book. Feel better now?

It's true though, isn't it? The more trials of life you go through, the more tempting it is to let another small piece of your heart die. Every year brings another trial, and thus it seems we lose more of our heart every time we add another candle to the cake and blow them out.

But what if it didn't have to be like this? What if God has made a way for us not to lose heart? Sure we know that God has redeemed us, given us a new heart, made us into new creations, and saved us for eternity – all through the gospel of Jesus Christ. While these truths may inspire us for a time when we first begin to learn about them, somehow those feelings of victory never seem to last. Life in a fallen world, Satan, and our own sinful flesh seem to keep finding new ways of knocking us down.

Jesus knows what we've been through and he knows what's ahead. He knows how easy it will be for us to give up. And so in kindness, he offers us a way out; or perhaps to say it a better way, he offers us a way through. He teaches us how to *never quit*.

Prayer. Yes, prayer. I know what you're thinking because I felt the same way when I began to ask the question, "How can I avoid losing heart? How can I avoid giving up?" As I felt God leading me to Luke 18:1, it seemed like another letdown to be offered such a Christian, cliché solution. Prayer? Really God? That's the secret sauce to living a life of victory?

As I pondered this question further and studied God's word, God began to crack my cynicism and made me realize what I know about prayer is not all there is to know, and more importantly what I *know* is not the same thing as what I *experience* in prayer. I began to realize that prayer is not only an endless subject to learn about, more importantly it is an endless opportunity to experience God in fresh, amazing ways all the time.

As God has narrowed my search on how to keep my heart alive by pointing me to this biblical, personal need for prayer, two words have begun to stick out: passion and power. As I look at the prayer life of Jesus, it becomes abundantly clear that his passion (which includes his consistency) and his power (which includes his impact) are otherworldly compared to my own.

If we could have passion and power in prayer, I believe our prayer life would begin to look a lot more like Jesus' prayer life. Perhaps more importantly, though, our life in general would begin to look a lot more like Jesus' life. If anyone had reason to lose heart, it was Jesus. He came to love the world, and all it did was betray him in return. But if anyone was fully alive, on fire for God, and living a life full of meaningful risk, adventure, and fruitfulness – if anyone had passion and power, surely it was Jesus Christ.

Which brings us to this little parable taught by Jesus in Luke 18:1-8 about a widow and an unjust judge. That's just so Jesus. I'm desperate for the secret to live with passion and power, and not only does he lead me back to something so common like prayer, he then explains the significance of prayer with a few lines about a desperate widow and an evil judge. Where are you going with this, Jesus?

Pray Always Because It Is the Secret to Not Losing Heart

I like to overcomplicate things. Let's go back into my childhood. Let's take a deep look into my thinking process. Let's analyze every word this person said to me. Na, Jesus says. Let's just start with prayer.

As I was going through seminary for pastoral counseling, I was taught a principle I believe Jesus practiced, "Complicated problems don't always require complicated solutions."

I think that's why it's so easy to blow past Luke 18:1, "And he told them a parable to the effect that they ought always to pray and not lose heart." To really appreciate what is being said here, we have to set the context at which Jesus is speaking these things.

In Luke 17:22, which is the beginning of the paragraph just before Luke 18:1, it states, "And [Jesus] said to the disciples, 'The days are coming when you will desire to see one of the days of the Son of Man, and you will not see it.'" He then goes on to explain that tough times are ahead. He's going to return to earth unexpectedly one day like a thief in the night, but before he does the earth is going to resemble the days of Noah and Lot (Luke 17:27-28). These men lived in evil times where the people hated God, thus seeking to live righteously in the lifetimes of Noah and Lot was extremely difficult. Jesus says all this to show his disciples their life is also going to get extremely hard.

As Luke 18:1 begins, it becomes clear that he is still talking to his disciples. So as we read through Luke 18:1-8, we have to remember that the audience of Jesus' parable is one that is dear to his heart. He's talking directly to the men he has a personal relationship with, whom he cares about deeply; and he is preparing these men for the most difficult season of their life. The time of the crucifixion is just around the corner. So how does Jesus prepare them? He teaches them the importance of prayer.

It's so uncomplicated we can skip right over it. But again, Jesus' intentions for this parable are unmistakable, "And he told them a parable to the effect that they ought always to pray and not lose heart" (Luke 18:1). The NIV translates "not lose heart" as "not give up." It seems we only have two options in life. Prayer or giving up.

Prayer is not a complicated solution, but that does not mean it can't solve our complicated problems. In fact, Jesus assures us it will.

Praying Is Not Only an Action, It Is a State of Being/Living

So we all agree that life is a challenge that makes us want to give up, lose heart, and live an uninspired existence. And now we know that Jesus tells us the solution to not giving up is prayer. But he doesn't tell us just to pray, he specifically tells us we "ought always to pray." Always? That seems a bit hyperbolic and exaggerated, no?

It would be easy to assume so if it were not for the fact that this same command is found all over Scripture. 1 Thessalonians 5:17 says, "pray without ceasing." Ephesians 6:18 explains that as we put on the full armor of God, we must do so while "praying at all times in the Spirit, with all prayer and supplication." Philippians 4:6 states that "in everything by prayer and supplication with thanksgiving let your requests be made known to

God." Colossians 4:2 adds, "Devote yourselves to prayer."

Not only are we explicitly told to "always pray," we are given this pattern and example from the men in the Bible. David penned, "My eyes are ever toward the LORD" (Psalm 25:15). Paul wrote "God . . . is my witness how constantly I remember you in my prayers at all times" (Romans 1:9-10). And certainly Jesus was in constant communication with the Father (John 11:42, John 12:49).

So what does this all mean? I don't think our employers will allow us to spend our whole work day in the closet praying. It wouldn't be helpful to your children if they lost their parents to the monastery. To talk only to God and not to people would make it impossible to love people, which is what God tells us to do.

These commands to "pray without ceasing" don't make sense unless you understand all that pray can be. Certainly we must set significant times aside to lie on our face, kneel at our bedside, or rock in our favorite chair as we commune with God. Of course there are certain types of prayers that we must sit down and actually do. Yes, we must open up the word of God and really pray the Scriptures and listen to the Holy Spirit apply the Bible personally to our life and heart.

But prayer can be more than all of these things. Praying can be a state of being, a way of living. There are many types of prayer: praise/thanksgiving, confession, intercession (prayers for others), supplication (prayers requests for self), and meditation/listening. But essentially, prayer can be simplified and be defined as communing with God. Or perhaps to say it a little less religiously: prayer is actively walking with God in a personal, moment to moment relationship. I can go on a walk with my wife and not say a word but still be in active relationship with her. (For more on this, see Brother Lawrence's book, *Practicing the Presence of God*.)

When we begin to understand the full scope of what prayer can be with God, suddenly Luke 18:1 begins to make a lot more sense. God. He's the solution. A rich, deep, profound, moment by moment relationship with the Father, Son, and Holy Spirit is exactly what our hearts need to stay alive. We were made to listen to him, to talk to him, and walk with him; but because of sin everything got messed up (Genesis 1-3). Ultimately we lose heart not because the world is hard to live in; we lose heart because we try to live in the world without God, which is more than hard . . . it's impossible.

As God began to show me all that I can have with him, that intimately walking with him is the solution my heart needs, my relief suddenly began to dampen as reality sat on my like a bully at recess. Well of course if I remain connected to God in prayer all the time my life will be rich and meaningful, but I struggle to pray for 5 minutes straight without being internally sidetracked by the many random thoughts that often run unchecked throughout my head. And not only is my attention limited, my motivation is lacking. Let's be honest, sometimes we just don't want to pray that much.

Jesus knows all this. Thankfully Luke 18:1-8 is not just a parable by Jesus to tell us that we should pray as much as possible. It's also a rich passage of Scripture Jesus has given us on how to do it. Luke 18:1 tells us what we ought to do, but then in Luke 18:2-8 Jesus teaches us how to do it.

Passionate, Powerful Prayer Is the Result of Seeing God Properly

Jesus loved to teach using parables. Stories have a knack for capturing our attention in deeper ways than logical arguments. Throughout his many parables, Jesus compared and contrasted characters in his stories with people and events which are (or were) in real life. A parable is different than an allegory, which is when every character and detail has an exact representative in real life. Parables have a main theme and lesson taught through the story, which means not every word always symbolizes something specific in our life, but the whole story has a general thrust that is meant to impact us in a specific way.

With that said, parables always compare *or* contrast something (or someone) in Jesus' story with something (or someone) in real life. In the case of the unjust judge, Jesus is simply *contrasting* this judge with God. Everything we will learn about this judge will take us into a deeper understanding of God by seeing how totally different God is compared to the unjust judge. And the deeper our understanding of God, the more passionate and powerful our prayers will become.

In Martin Loyd-Jone's book called *Revival*, he states, "Great prayer is always the outcome of great understanding. . . . It is when a man is in the furnace of affliction, it is then, indeed, that he falls back upon certain fundamental truths of which he is absolutely sure and certain. The key to great praying is a deep knowledge and grasp of the doctrine of grace."

As we will learn throughout this short book, to respond to God properly, we must see him accurately. Humans are responders. What we see, think, and believe will dictate how we live, act, and pray. For example, John 12:41 explains, "Isaiah said these things because he saw [God's] glory and spoke of him." Because Isaiah saw God clearly, he then spoke of him boldly.

David wrote, "My eyes are ever toward the Lord, for he will pluck my feet out of the net" (Psalm 25:15). Because David *knew* that only God could rescue him from trials, he was then motivated to keep his eyes always on the Lord. Again David states, "And those who know your name put their trust in you" (Psalm 9:10). God's name reveals his character, and thus those who *know* God's character respond properly by putting their trust in him.

On the flipside, our poor responses and sins are always a result of believing falsely about God. When we don't see him as he truly is, when we don't understand God's character as he intends us to, or when we allow the problems of the world to block out our view of God's power, that's when our response to God begins to falter. Worship will not produce awe and wonder for God. Worship is always a response to the awe and wonder that is produced when we see God clearly.

The level of our time in prayer is the expression of the amount of active belief we truly have in God. Do you believe God cares for you? Do you believe God hears you and speaks back to you? Do you believe God is all powerful, able to handle anything you pray about? Do you believe that the end of this story is already written for victory, therefore we can trust him even if there are unknown pages ahead?

The answers to these questions will not be found in our verbal answers. The answers to these questions will be revealed through our time spent, or lack of time spent, in prayer.

Thus to help us in our prayers so we will not lose heart, Jesus first helps us see God more clearly. He knows that if he is going to help us "always pray and not lose heart," we are going to have see a grand vision of God as he actually is so it will elicit a grand, life changing response expressed in our prayer life.

If we hope to never quit, we have to believe this bedrock truth deeply – that God is good.

Questions:

1. Why do you think people "lose heart" and why is prayer so important in keeping our hearts alive? Explain.

2. "Complicated problems don't always require complicated solutions." Do you agree with this phrase? Why or why not?

3. In Luke 18:1, who is Jesus talking to and what is the context for why Jesus told them this parable? (Read Luke 17:20-37 for assistance.)

4. How would you define what prayer is? What are some types of prayer that you know about (asking, praying Scripture, etc.)?

5. Read 1 Thessalonians 5:17, Ephesians 6:18, Philippians 4:6, Colossians 4:2, and Psalm 16:7-8. What do these verses have in common? What can you learn from these passages of Scripture?

6. David penned, "My eyes are ever toward the LORD" (Psalm 25:15). Moses requested that God's presence would always be with him (Exodus 33:13-16). And certainly Jesus was in constant communication with the Father (John 11:42, John 12:49). Who is someone you admire (in the Bible, in history, or someone you know) and what is their relationship with God like?

7. What is a parable? In Luke 18:1-8, how should we look at the unjust judge to learn more about God?

8. How do our beliefs about God affect our prayers? Give some examples.

9. What's Jesus goal in teaching us this parable? How will learning about this unjust judge and this widow affect our prayer life?

10. No matter how strong our prayer life is, we can always pray with more passion and power. What obstacles keep you from praying more often? Write down a prayer asking God to help you with these specific barriers.

Week 2: Believe God Is Completely Good

He said, "In a certain city there was a judge who neither feared God nor respected man." – Luke 18:2

Luke 18:1 makes it known that Jesus wants us to always be in communion with God. He then instantly motivates us in Luke 18:2 to passionately pursue this relationship by giving us a picture of God's absolute goodness, holiness, and love.

The first thing we learn about this judge is that he is as wicked as can be. He is totally depraved to the maximum. It may not seem like a big deal that this judge "neither feared God nor cared about men" (NIV), but Jesus states these two very specific traits because he is showing that this unjust judge is breaking the two greatest commandments. In Matthew 22:36-40 Jesus is asked what is the greatest commandment in all the Law. He replied:

> "You shall love the Lord your God with all your heart and with all your soul and with all your mind. This is the great and first commandment. And a second is like it: You shall love your neighbor as yourself. On these two commandments depend all the Law and the Prophets."

So this judge is completely unholy and unloving to the max because he doesn't love God and doesn't love people, thus he is breaking the heart behind the entire Law. But remember, the whole point of Jesus' parable is to show us how God is totally different than this unjust judge. Jesus points out the bad and corrupt character of the judge to highlight the totally good and pure character of God.

Additionally, the fact that Jesus created a story where a man is being dishonoring to a widow, again, is showing how different this judge is compared to God. In Exodus 22:22-24, God says, "You shall not mistreat any widow or fatherless child. If you do mistreat them, and they cry out to me, I will surely hear their cry, and my wrath will burn . . . ."

By highlighting the wickedness of this judge who abuses a widow, Jesus is underscoring God's awesome graciousness and compassion for the weak. Why does God have such a heart for widows and orphans? Because God has a heart for all people in need, and widows and orphans are in great need. Spiritually speaking though, this passion God has for widows is applied to us all, for we are all weak and in desperate need of his protection. We have no one else but him.

If Jesus' whole goal in this parable is to get us to pray all the time so we don't lose heart (Luke 18:1), and now in Luke 18:2 Jesus makes it abundantly clear how good God really is, then knowing God is good must be essential to our pursuit of him. It's a truth you may have heard since Sunday school, but at the foundation to a passionate and powerful prayer life is the belief that God really does care for you.

Pray Always Because God Is Good

"Oh give thanks to the LORD, for he is good, for his steadfast love endures forever!" (Psalm 107:1). "For" means "because." The reason, therefore, we are to be motivated to give thanks to God is *because* we know that his love endures forever.

If you don't know his love for you endures forever, you won't give him the constant thanks he deserves. If you don't believe in the goodness of God, you will never have the motivation to come and pray to him always. If you think God is out to get you, out to punish you, or simply out there not thinking about you, you will never have a strong desire to pursue him.

It doesn't take a relationship expert to know that if a girl never gives the guy a second look when he continually pursues her, eventually he is going to stop pursuing her. Even if she does like him but he doesn't know it, he is going to stop the pursuit. No one gravitates towards someone who is cruel. This is why knowing God is good and that he deeply cares about you is pivotal to your passion for him.

Mary was a woman known for her passion to simply love Jesus. In John 12:1-8 we see her take expensive perfume worth a whole year's wages and pour it on the feet of Jesus as she then wipes his feet with her hair. Now that's the type of pursuit Jesus tells us to have in Luke 18:1 so we don't lose heart.

What's important to note is that in John 11 Jesus just got done raising Mary's brother Lazarus from the dead. Mary's great act of lavish love was a response to the great act of love she just witnessed by Jesus. She could love Jesus much because she saw and understood the great love of Jesus for her and her family. As 1 John 4:19 explains, "We love him because he first loved us." 2 Corinthians 5:14 (NIV) adds, "For Christ's love compels us . . . ."

To love God and pray to him always, you must keep his love for you at the forefront of your mind and heart. If you keep forgetting to pray, it's probably because you keep forgetting how much God loves you.

Paul says in Romans 12:1, "Therefore, I urge you, brothers, in view of God's mercy, to offer your bodies as living sacrifices, holy and pleasing to God – this is your spiritual act of worship." Romans 12:1 starts with "Therefore" because the first eleven chapters of Romans were a thorough explanation of the great love of God expressed through the gospel of Jesus Christ. Paul's urging us to worship, but he is motivating us with the phrase "in view of God's mercy." This means we should look at the mercy of God which should then cause us to worship.

The King's James Bible translates phrase "spiritual act of worship" as "*which is* your reasonable service." When you look at what Christ did for us, it is only reasonable that we worship him and seek him wholeheartedly. If you don't constantly look at God's love for you expressed in the gospel of Jesus Christ, you will have no inner urge to pursue him passionately.

Notice that in the beginning of most of the letters by Paul, he spends significant time first expressing his love and affection for the audience he is writing to. Most Bible translations put the headings "Greeting" and then "Thanksgiving" in Chapter 1 in many of Paul's letters. Paul was very knowledgeable and very bold in his counsel. Through his letters, he counseled in a straightforward, no fuss type of way. But before he counseled, he made sure the people knew he cared.

However, in 1 Timothy and Titus, Paul's letters to other pastors he was mentoring, he skips the "Thanksgiving" section. Perhaps he does this here because he already has such a solid, preexisting relationship with these men. He knows they know he loves them, so he can just jump right into the counseling part.

Pray Always Because God Is a Good Father Who Desires to Bless You

Perhaps the caring heart and character of God is the first lesson Jesus teaches us about in this parable because this is foundational to our desire in pursuing the Lord. If we don't know he cares for us, why would we pray to him?

1 Peter 5:7 (NIV) states, "Cast all your anxiety on him because he cares for you." Peter motivates us to cast all our troubles onto the Lord by reminding us that God really does care. God really is good. If you don't know he cares for you, if you don't know that the heart of God is for you, or if you doubt the goodness of God, you won't pray very much.

In Dr. Dobson's book called *Brining Up Boys*, he instructs that during the teen years, kids will find it much harder to listen to the advice of their parents if they felt unloved in childhood. He instructs parents, "The best way to avoid this teenage time bomb is to diffuse it in childhood . . . Begin now to build a relationship that will see you through the storms of adolescence." Dr. Leman, in *Parenting Your Powerful Child*, also states, "They don't care what you know . . . until they know that you care."

Just like a child who rebels against her parents because she doubts their love for her, if we don't believe deep in our being that God really cares for us, we will find it very hard to "always pray" and thus we will lose heart and give up (Luke 18:1). In Matthew 7:7-11, Jesus uses this parent-to-child metaphor by again contrasting our totally good Heavenly Father with sinful fathers on earth:

> "Ask, and it will be given to you; seek, and you will find; knock, and it will be opened to you. For everyone who asks receives, and the one who seeks finds, and to the one who knocks it will be opened. Or which one of you, if his son asks him for bread, will give him a stone? Or if he asks for a fish, will give him a serpent? If you then, who are evil, know how to give good gifts to your children, how much more will your Father who is in heaven give good things to those who ask him!"

Here Jesus is telling us to consistently ask, to continually seek, and to constantly knock – all of these being prayer metaphors. To motivate us to pray like this, however, he points out the goodness of our Heavenly Father. Jesus says, "If you then, who are evil, know how to give good gifts to your children, how much more will your Father who is in heaven give good things to those who ask him!" (Matthew 7:11). Jesus highlights the evil of earthly fathers not to bash them but to highlight how good our Heavenly Father is. If our earthly dads were able to give us good gifts, how much more will our Heavenly Father be able to do even better?

Jesus wants us to be blessed, but he knows oftentimes God won't bless us until we ask him. And he knows we won't ask him until we know that our heavenly Father really is good and really does desire to give us good gifts. So many times we just need to ask, "You do not have, because you do not ask" (James 4:2). But Jesus knows we won't ask anything from our Father if we don't believe he desires to bless us.

I recently heard of an old tradition that Amish parents have when one of their children runs away from home. I'm certainly not in favor of everything the Amish believe, but I think this particular tradition they have is especially beautiful. When one of their children runs away from home the parents set a place at the table for their run away child at breakfast, lunch, and dinner. They put out a plate, the silverware, a cup, the whole thing. But no one sits in the chair. They just leave the spot empty.

Since this is a tradition, the Amish run-away knows their family back home is setting a place for them. So at least three times a day the run-away will be forced to remember the love their family still has for them. The parents want their children to know that at any point they want to come home, there will always be a place waiting for them at the table. Why do the parents do this? Because no one comes home when they believe they are unwanted.

You see? Jesus is trying to motivate us to always pray and come back home to the Father by reminding us of the great and perfect love of God. The judge was bad to the uttermost, not fearing God and not caring about people. God is good to the uttermost, putting his glory above all else and caring for people with all of his heart.

No matter where we go, no matter what kind of crazy we have created in our lives, Jesus wants us to know God is totally good and loving, thus we should pray to him all the time, always returning, never quitting.

Questions:

1. Read Luke 18:2 and Matthew 22:36-40. What do we now know about this unjust judge?

2. Why is it especially bad that this judge is treating a widow like this?

3. Look at the things you listed in question 1 and 2 about this unjust judge. If Jesus is contrasting the unjust judge with God, what can you now infer about God?

4. Why is it so important to really believe that God is good if you want to have a strong prayer life?

5. Read John 12:1-8. Why were Mary, Martha, and Lazarus so willing to celebrate Jesus? Why was Judas so resistant to love Jesus like them?

6. Read 1 John 4:19, 2 Corinthians 5:14-15, and Luke 7:47. What do these verses have in common?

7. 1 Peter 5:7 (NIV) states, "Cast all your anxiety on him because he cares for you." In a parent to child relationship, why is it so important that the child knows the parent loves him or her? How does this relate to your relationship with the Heavenly Father?

8. Jesus said, "If you then, who are evil, know how to give good gifts to your children, how much more will your Father who is in heaven give good things to those who ask him!" (Matthew 7:11). What does God give and who does he give it to?

9. Sometimes we can know "God is good" theologically but we can struggle to believe it personally. Do you find it easy or hard to believe that God is good? Explain why.

10. How can you increase your belief in the goodness of God? (Perhaps share some of the struggles you listed in question 9 and ask others in the group for ideas on how to overcome these struggles.)

Week 3: Believe God Hears and Speaks

*And there was a widow in that city who kept coming to him and saying, "Give me justice against my adversary."
⁴ For a while he refused, but afterward he said to himself, "Though I neither fear God nor respect man,
⁵ yet because this widow keeps bothering me, I will give her justice, so that she will not beat me down by her continual coming." –Luke 18:3-5*

The unjust judge's lack of love and goodness is shown by his motivation in granting the widow's request. He doesn't grant it for her; he actually grants the request for himself.

The unjust judge grants the request so the widow will leave him alone. God grants our requests so we will keep coming. The unjust judge refused her for some time, but God will answer people quickly (Luke 18:8). The unjust judge answers her request because the woman worked so hard and annoyed him. God answers prayers because of his grace, because of his character, because he loves us, and not because of our efforts and moral striving. Unlike the unjust judge, God actually wants us to come to him and he wants to speak to us.

Notice that in this whole exchange, the unjust judge doesn't even talk to the widow; he never actually says anything directly to her. Luke 18:4 states "For some time he refused. But finally he said to himself . . . ." The widow pleads day after day, but the judge never verbally says anything back to her. Sadly, this is how many of us have come to view God, a powerful yet silent person who may or may not be listening. It's impossible to want to pray if you think God does not want to hear from you. The more deeply you believe that God does want to hear from you, the more your passion to pray will increase.

Jesus wants us to pray always and not lose heart. Therefore he knows how crucial it is that we really believe God is listening and that he speaks personally to us. Jesus contrasts God with a silent, unjust judge because he knows that we will never talk to God if we believe he is like that. Jesus knows we will lose heart if we don't personally connect to the heart of God in conversation. He knows we will never listen to hear God if we believe he would never waste his time confiding in us.

Pray Always Because God Is Always Listening and Speaking

Psalm 25:8-9, 14 explains, "Good and upright is the Lord; therefore he instructs sinners in his ways. He guides the humble in what is right and teaches them his way. . . The Lord confides in those who fear him; he makes his covenant known to them." God desires to speak to us. Even though we are sinful, he instructs us in his ways. When we approach God through Jesus Christ, fearing him and honoring him as we must, God gives us friendship with himself and even "confides" in us.

God is anything but an angry, aloof person seeking to avoid conversation with humans. He sent his Son to earth for the purpose of reconnecting your heart with his.

I know it can be hard to believe sometimes, but this is one of the many reasons it is so utterly crucial our understanding of God is based first on Scripture and nothing else. Our experiences mislead us, our opinions really don't matter, and the world's wisdom is usually ridiculous. Contrary to whatever else we have come to believe, and no matter how we've come to believe it, the Bible makes it clear that God listens to our prayers and speaks to us personally in our hearts through his word and Spirit:

> Psalm 16:7, "I bless the LORD who gives me counsel."

> Romans 5:2-3, "Therefore, since we have been justified by faith, we have peace with God through our Lord Jesus Christ. Through him we have also obtained access by faith into this grace in which we stand, and we rejoice in hope of the glory of God."

> Romans 5:5, "God's love has been poured into our hearts through the Holy Spirit who has been given to us."

> Romans 8:26, "Likewise the Spirit helps us in our weakness. For we do not know what to pray for as we ought, but the Spirit himself intercedes for us with groanings too deep for words."

John 10:27, "My sheep hear my voice, and I know them, and they follow me."

Hebrews 1:1-2, "Long ago, at many times and in many ways, God spoke to our fathers by the prophets, but in these last days he has spoken to us by his Son, whom he appointed the heir of all things, through whom also he created the world."

Ephesians 2:13, 18, "But now in Christ Jesus you who once were far off have been brought near by the blood of Christ. . . For through him we both have access in one Spirit to the Father."

1 Corinthians 2:11-13, "So also no one comprehends the thoughts of God except the Spirit of God. Now we have received not the spirit of the world, but the Spirit who is from God, that we might understand the things freely given us by God. And we impart this in words not taught by human wisdom but taught by the Spirit, interpreting spiritual truths to those who are spiritual."

God will never say anything to you that would contradict what he has already spoken to us all through his Spirit in the word of God. But clearly God, through his Spirit and his word, speak to us personally. (For more on this, read the book, *Hearing God*, by Dallas Willard)

Always Pray to Your Father Because He Is Always Fathering You

By God's grace I have had the opportunity to do missionary work in Liberia, West Africa. During my time there I had the privilege of visiting a lot of orphanages, some on a weekly basis. I saw hundreds of orphan children. Babies, toddlers, children, teenagers. Some well fed, some not so well fed. Some with beds to sleep in and roofs over their heads, some without. Some of these orphans were in the city, some were way out in the African bush. Some were healthy and loved to play, some were crippled and lame.

I remember one boy named Francis. He was probably around fourteen, but he didn't know his true birth date because his parents died when he was young and no one was there to share the details of his early life, a common problem amongst orphan children. Francis was a free spirit and did not like the rules and expectations of an orphanage, so he lived in a shipping container in the port, wheeling and dealing with the sailors to provide food for himself. Just from talking to all the sailors from different countries he had learned multiple languages: English, Russian, Ukrainian, French . . . Francis could speak them all. He was a genius.

I remember visiting the orphans at HIV/Aids hospice. Some were just a shell of a human being, nothing but skin and bones. I remember one baby girl there, her name was "Princess." She couldn't have been more than five or six months old. She had the AIDS virus and was blind. As she sat on my lap, she felt my arm and hand with her fingernail, becoming acquainted with me the only way she could.

I saw many, many different types of orphans doing many different things during my time in Africa. But there is one thing I can't remember seeing any orphan do. In all my time there I saw them playing, laughing, fighting, silent, sick, speaking multiple languages, blind with AIDS – but what I never saw was crying.

I can't remember not one orphan crying. Every normal kid cries for something or other, and you'd think kids with these types of lives would cry the most. But the sad truth is that orphans don't cry because they learn from an early age no one is listening. No matter how long or hard they cry, no one comes.

The people who ran the orphanages were extremely loving people from what I saw, but the ratio was around 100 kids to every 2 adults. Even if they wanted to help a crying child there simply was not enough hands to go around. And so you could go into a room full of infant orphans and it would be dead silent because those orphans knew they were alone and no one was coming. It was truly heartbreaking.

Do you see why Jesus makes the point to show how different God is compared to this silent judge? The unjust judge doesn't say a word to the widow. She doesn't know if he's listening or not. Jesus is trying to show us that God is nothing like this. You're not alone in this world. God has not abandoned you. Thus, unlike an orphan with no one to listen, we should cry out to God day and night because he is listening day and night. We should pray to our Father always because he is always there fathering us. We should never give up and lose heart because God is always seeking to strengthen and love us, to lead and guide us. Psalm 139:4-14 state:

> "Before a word is on my tongue you, LORD, know it completely. . . .Where can I go from your Spirit? Where can I flee from your presence? If I go up to the heavens, you are there; if I make my bed in the depths, you are there. If I rise on the wings of the dawn, if I settle on the far side of the sea, even there your hand will guide me, your right hand will hold me fast. If I say, "Surely the darkness will hide me and the light become night around me," even the darkness will not be dark to you; the night will shine like the day, for darkness is as light to you. For you created my inmost being; you knit me together in my mother's womb. I praise you because I am fearfully and wonderfully made; your works are wonderful, I know that full well."

Why does the psalmist praise God? The psalmist praises God because he knows God is always there with him, loving him deeply. You will never worship and pray to God always if you do not believe his presence is always with you.

Do you know there is not one verse in the Bible about God not hearing the prayers of his children? He may tell us to wait, or he may say a gentle no, but he never just ignores us. There's no example of even the smallest prayer accidentally just slipping by him. Matthew 7:8 says, "For everyone who asks receives; he who seeks finds, and to him who knocks the door will be opened."

This is the very reason Jesus came to earth to begin with. God knew that in our sin, we could not come to him as he desired (Psalm 66:18, Romans 5:8). He sought to show his great love by coming in the flesh, dying on the cross, and being raised from the dead so that if we believe in him and follow him, we shall have everlasting life *with him* (John 14:2, John 17:3).

John 1:14, 18 (NLT) states, "So the Word became human and made his home among us. He was full of unfailing love and faithfulness. . . No one has ever seen God. But the unique One, who is himself God, is near to the Father's heart. He has revealed God to us." Since Jesus is himself God, and since Jesus was made human and then made his home among other humans, it is undeniable that God really does desire a relationship with people. Jesus is "near to the Father's heart" and came to bring us near too.

God could have sent Jesus into the world as an aloof, desert-wondering-monk and then sacrificed him in the wilderness somewhere with no one knowing it. This would have still fulfilled the necessity for a perfect atoning sacrifice needed to get his people into heaven, but it would have been without the intimacy Jesus offered throughout his life.

As we know, Jesus came teaching, healing, and living among the lost people of the world. If you want to do an interesting Bible study, simply read through the gospels and note every time Jesus touched someone or was touched by someone. He came to earth not to offer a lifeless, loveless religion, but a relationship with himself based upon his kindness. His earthly ministry was skin-to-skin because he actually *wants* to be with the people he loves. It's not a burden to him. It's his desire to be near to us.

Jesus gave us a look into the thoughts of the judge who said, "because this widow keeps bothering me, I will give her justice, so that she will not beat me down by her continual coming" (Luke 18:5). Jesus pointed this out so we will know God feels the exact opposite way about us. He never gets tired of hearing from you. He answerers your prayers because he loves when you come to him. The judge wanted the widow to come to him less, but God wants you to come to him more and more. Jesus came to earth to draw the lost to himself by showing us in a personal, intimate way how much he cares for us. Jeremiah 31:3 (NIV) says, "I have loved you with an everlasting love; I have drawn you with unfailing kindness."

Through his Spirit using the hands of men, God made the Bible so we could know the life of Jesus intimately and all that he did on earth. He didn't have to leave us such a great, detailed account of how loving Jesus was on earth. But God made sure it was all recorded for the ages to come because he wants us all to know him personally and intimately. He wants us all to know that when you come into a personal relationship with God through the gospel, you too will experience this intimacy that Jesus constantly offered to people.

So in this parable about a widow and an unjust judge, up to this point Jesus has sought to motivate us to "always pray" by showing us what God is really like (Luke 18:1), by showing us that he cares for us (Luke

18:2), and by showing us that God really is listening and eager for us to hear him speak personally (Luke 18:3-5).

In short, Jesus has taught us we should always pray and not give up because God truly loves us. In the verses ahead, however, not only does Jesus focus on the love of God, he also focuses on the great power and sovereignty of God as well.

Questions:

1. Why does the unjust judge finally grant the widow her request? What was his motivation?

2. Why does God grant us our requests? What is his motivation?

3. Luke 18:4 says of the unjust judge, "For a while he refused, but afterward he said to himself...." What can you learn about God from this verse?

4. Why is it so important that Scripture guides our beliefs about God rather than allowing our feelings to guide our beliefs about God? Secondly, how do beliefs affect our feelings?

5. Read Romans 8:26, John 10:27, Hebrews 1:1-2, and Ephesians 2:13, 18. Summarize in your own words the truths expressed in these verses.

6. Read Psalm 139:4-14. What does this passage teach us about God?

7. What does the Incarnation of Jesus (1 John 1:14, 18) reveal about God's desire towards us?

8. Does God answer our prayers because we ask him over and over again? Explain your answer.

9. God is love (1 John 4:8). But what is love? Read all of 1 Corinthians 13, paying special attention to verses 4-8. Summarize in your own words what love is.

10. What's one new thing you learned after reading this chapter? (If you didn't learn anything new, what's one good reminder that you got from this chapter?)

Week 4: Believe God Is All Powerful

*And the Lord said, "Hear what the unrighteous judge
says. ⁷ And will not God give justice to his elect, who cry
to him day and night? Will he delay long over them?
– Luke 18:6-7*

The NIV translates Luke 18:7 as "And will not God bring
about justice for his chosen ones, who cry out to him
day and night?" God literally "brings about" things. The
Greek word for "bring about" (NIV) and "give" (ESV) is
"poieo" and means, "To form, produce, or to cause."

God is in the business of creating. In the beginning of
Genesis God made something out of nothing with the
words of his mouth. He spoke trillions of stars and
galaxies into existence with just a few words. He spoke
into existence all the land and all the plant life and all
the thousands of species in the animal kingdom. God
literally made human beings out of the dust of the
ground. Everything that we see, God has brought
about. As Hebrews 11:3 states, "By faith we understand
that the universe was created by the word of God, so
that what is seen was not made out of things that are
visible."

So when Jesus states that God can "bring about justice
for his chosen ones," he really means it. God is totally
sovereign and supreme in every way. And Jesus is
seeking to draw our attention to his power so that it
will motivate us to love him and pray to him always. If
God created everything and can create anything, why

wouldn't we pray to him always? God brings about whatever he wants, so much so that he even has a chosen, elected people.

Jesus said in Luke 18:7, "And will not God give justice to his elect." Often times when people hear that God chooses and elects people, they get their theological underwear all wedged up and say philosophical things like, "Well if God chooses and elects and has the power to do whatever he wants, why should we evangelize. If he elects us, how do we have free will? If he chooses people, why should we pray for their salvation at all?"

But Jesus is bringing God's sovereignty to our attention so it will have the exact opposite effect on us. The fact that God does have the power to bring about what he desires is the very reason why we should pray to him at all. Everyone who prays to God, whether they would verbalize it this way or not, is showing by their prayers that they believe in the sovereignty of God to "choose" and "elect" and "bring about" what he wants.

No one would pray for lost people's salvation, or about anything at all for that matter, if they believed God was powerless to do something about it. If we really all believed that everything depended on the free choices of man only, no one would pray to God. If we believed everything that happened was because man was in total control of the outcome, prayer would not exist.

Pray Always Because God Is All Powerful

Perhaps we are on to something here. We know that prayer is a real biblical category that all Christians should participate in. But we also know that it is a challenge to "always pray and not lose heart" (Luke 18:1).

One explanation for our lack of prayer is our lack of belief in the sovereignty of God. The more you emphasize the power of man, the less prayer makes sense. At the core of prayer is the idea that we are talking with God because he is the only one powerful enough to do anything about the needs being discussed in the prayers. If you subtract the first premise (God is powerful enough to actually do whatever he wants), then the second logical premise evaporates too (that we should pray to him). If God isn't powerful, we shouldn't pray. If God is powerful, we should pray.

Jesus draws our attention to the total, sovereign power of God in order to help us "always pray and not give up" (Luke 18:1). Jesus reminds us that God "brings about" things and has an "elect" people (Luke 18:7). Therefore, the fact that God does have the power to choose people and bring about things is the very reason we should cry out to him day and night.

The biblical truth that God is in control of everything should not deflate your prayer life and cause you to pray less, it should cause you to pray more, with more confidence, because if God was powerless to do whatever he wanted, why pray at all? Prayer to God would be foolish if man was in total control. Praying is a confession that you do believe in the power of God. So if you find yourself struggling to pray, perhaps it because you have overemphasized the power of man and underemphasized the power of God to move on your behalf.

In J.I. Packer's book, *Evangelism and the Sovereignty of God*, he addresses the logical roadblocks that occur when we embrace God's election and then struggle to see the point of evangelizing. The logic goes something like this, "If the only way to be saved is to be chosen, then who cares if we tell people about Jesus anyway?"

Throughout Packer's book, he makes the point that God's sovereignty is not a reason to evangelize less. It is the reason to evangelize more. Because God does change the heart of sinners is the only reason we should evangelize. I'll let you read the book on your own to hear his full arguments, but how he begin in his opening chapter relates perfectly to our subject at hand:

> "I do not intend to spend any time at all proving to you the general truth that *God is sovereign in His world*. There is no need; for I know that, if you are a Christian, you believe this already. How do I know that? Because I know that, if you are a Christian, you pray; and the recognition of God's sovereignty is the basis of your prayers. In prayer, you ask for things and give thanks for things. Why? Because you recognize that God is the author and source of all the good that you have had already, and all the good that you hope for in the future. This is the fundamental philosophy of Christian prayer. . . In effect, therefore, what we do every time we pray is to confess our own impotence and God's

sovereignty. The very fact that a Christian prays is thus proof positive that he believes in the Lordship of his God."

Let me now take Packer's point a step further. If prayer "is to confess our own impotence and God's sovereignty," is it not safe to also say that a lack of prayer is to confess our unbiblical belief of our own power and God's impotence? Our beliefs about God will manifest in our prayer life. Again, therefore, Jesus seeks to help us always pray (Luke 18:1) by reestablishing the fundamental doctrine that makes prayer make any sense at all – that God is sovereign (Luke 18:7).

Again, Jesus said in Luke 18:6-7, "Hear what the unrighteous judge says. And will not God give justice to his elect, who cry to him day and night? Will he delay long over them?" Jesus is seeking to bolster our passion for prayer by reminding us of who alone holds the power to "give" anything.

The judge answered the widow's request because she kept coming to him again and again. God wants us to come to him again and again because he quickly answers our requests. We are not chosen because we pray. Rather, we must pray because we are chosen. God doesn't answer our prayers because of anything we do. Rather, what we do should be in response to our belief that God really answers prayer. God does not elect people because we cry out to him day and night. Rather, because Christians are his elect people we should cry out to him day and night.

In Matthew 6:9 when Jesus teaches us the Lord's Prayer, the first line in the prayer is "Our Father in heaven." Jesus is seeking to remind us that we should pray because our Father is reigning over the earth, able to bring about whatever he wills as he sits on his throne in heaven. "Our Father" is an intimate term, motivating us to pray because of God's fatherly love for us. Jesus covers the truth of God's love in Luke 18:2-5. But the next phrase, "who art in heaven," shows God's supremacy. Jesus covers the truth of God's power in Luke 18:6-7, motivating us to pray because of God's authority as the Preeminent King over all of his creation. Both facts, God's love and power, should motivate us to pray.

In the Lord's Prayer, Jesus then says "Your kingdom come, your will be done, on earth as it is in heaven" (Matthew 6:10). Jesus' prayer would make no sense if God could not actually bring about his will and his kingdom on earth.

Humans Are Not Enslaved Robots, But We Are Helpless Widows

When we begin to learn about God's sovereignty, the temptation is to turn into the "frozen chosen" who use God's power as excuse to be lazy. But as we have discussed, God's sovereignty is not a reason to pray less, work less, evangelize less — God's sovereignty should motivate us to do all of these things more. Because he is powerful, we step out in faith.

The other common response to learning about God's sovereignty is to feel like a mindless robot with no freedom. A God with complete control seems oppressive. But God wants us to feel the opposite. The Bible nowhere says that because God is sovereign, man is not free. Again, the opposite is true. Because God is sovereign, man can be free.

When God saves us through the gospel, he doesn't violate our freewill. He sets our will free. We are slaves to sin until Jesus sets us free (Romans 6:20-23). When Jesus sets us free, then we *freely choose* to follow a new Master. Galatians 5:1, "For freedom Christ has set us free; stand firm therefore, and do not submit again to a yoke of slavery." Because Christ has set us free now we must willfully choose to live free, actively choosing to not live under a yoke of slavery.

So in Luke 18:6-7, Jesus is not trying to say everyone is a robot with no freedom. But what he is saying is that everyone is like a helpless widow who is totally depended upon God for anything good in their lives.

You see, a widow in the times of Jesus would have been totally helpless in this male dominated society. History shows that widows were not even allowed to be in the courtroom unless there was absolutely no male who could plead her case. So for this widow to be coming to the judge herself in Jesus' parable, it meant not only did she have no husband, it meant she had no son, no brother, no uncle, no nephew, no distant male cousin . . . she literally had no one to plead her case on her behalf. She was the most destitute type of person in all of society. She had no hope to gain justice against her adversary except for this judge.

If the judge did not act on her behalf, she was completely helpless. And Jesus is trying to point out that in reality, we are this widow. Without God showing his kindness, we would have nothing. We are as powerless spiritually as this widow was physically.

This is perfect picture of the gospel. Romans 3:23 states that all have sinned and fallen short of the glory of God. Romans 8:8 states, "Those who are in the flesh cannot please God." We are all as totally helpless and in need of an advocate as this widow. Just as this widow will remain unjustified without someone helping her, we too would be unjustified without God moving on our behalf through the work of Christ (Romans 8:30). The clear, simple, and true message of the Bible is that everything good we have is from God, not ourselves:

> Acts 17:25 (NIV), "And [God] is not served by human hands, as if he needed anything. Rather, he himself gives everyone life and breath and everything else."

> James 1:16-17 (NIV), "Don't be deceived, my dear brothers and sisters. Every good and perfect gift is from above, coming down from the Father."

The widow understood that her hope was in the hands of the judge, just as we must understand our hope is truly in the hands of God alone. Notice what the widow did not do. She did not seek justice in her own power. She didn't turn to others once the judge refused her. Why? Because she understood that only the judge had the rightful authority to do anything about her problem. She wasn't going to take her eyes off the judge because she knew he was the only one who could truly help.

Likewise, when we begin to understand the great power of God and begin to truly believe he alone is sovereign and sufficient, that he alone has the authority to answer our deepest needs, only when we truly understand how destitute we are like this widow and how powerful God truly is – only then will we cry out to him day and night.

Only when we see him rightly will we seek him rightly. The greater our comprehension of his greatness and our lowness, the greater our capacity will be to seek him. If you want a powerful prayer life, you need to first realize how weak you are in your own strength. You know what kind of view of God you have by the health of your prayer life. Again, as we mentioned in Chapter 1, Dr. Martin Loyd-Jones said, "Great prayer is always the outcome of great understanding."

The widow is our example, for she was humble enough to know her helplessness. She went to the judge constantly because she knew she was powerless. We too should go to God constantly because we too must realize that without Christ, we really are helpless. A lack of consistent prayer to God is the surest sign of pride in one's self and doubt in God's power.

At the beginning of this book we said that if we hope to always pray and not lose heart, we will need to have passion and power like Jesus did in his prayer life. So far we have learned that we can have a *passionate* prayer life when we believe deeply that God loves us and is all powerful. We have also discussed how our prayer life can be *powerful* because we are praying to the only sovereign God who "brings about" whatever he wants.

In Luke 18:8, Jesus goes on to strengthen our belief in God's sovereignty by not only explaining that God has the power to change our present, but he is so powerful he has already written the future.

And when we align our prayers with the predetermined will of God, then our prayers become immensely powerful.

Questions:

1. How does remembering that God is The Creator (Genesis 1:1, Hebrews 11:3) affect our prayer life?

2. We can often get mixed emotions when we think about the sovereignty of God. How does it make you feel when you think about God being in total control?

3. While this study is not the place for a long debate about the relationship between man's free will and God's sovereignty, how should our belief in God's sovereignty affect our free choice to pray or not pray? In other words, should we pray less or more when we believe that God is in control? Explain.

4. The Lord's Prayer (Matthew 6:9-13) is one of the best places to look if you want to know how to pray. Read the first line of this prayer (Matthew 6:9). What does this teach you about God and prayer?

5. When we think of God's sovereignty, many people start to think of humans as robots. But that's not the analogy Jesus used. He compared humans to a widow. What does this widow in Luke 18 teach us about human power in relation to God's power?

6. Read Galatians 5:1. Why should Christians live free?

7. Read Acts 17:24-25 and James 1:16-17. Summarize in your own words what these verses say.

8. How does pride and an over emphasis on the power of humans affect our prayer life? Explain.

9. Read 2 Corinthians 12:7-10. How should your awareness of your weaknesses affect your prayer life?

10. We all struggle with pride at certain points in life. When do you personally start becoming prideful? What can you do to prevent pride and promote humility in your life?

Week 5: Believe God Wins

"I tell you, he will give justice to them speedily. Nevertheless, when the Son of Man comes, will he find faith on earth?" – Luke 18:8

My son has an adversary. She's red headed, immature, easily excitable, really fun, slobbery, and super annoying when she wants to play. His adversary also happens to be our golden retriever, Lois.

In typical first born fashion, my son wants to be in charge, and Lois is an easy target. "Lois, get off my toys! Lois, stop hitting me with your tail! Lois, stop barking! Lois, stop breathing on me!" The funny thing is Lois doesn't pay attention to him at all. She just keeps doing what she's doing as though he isn't shouting at the top of his lungs right in her unimpressed face.

It's not that she doesn't understand him; I think she finds pleasure in doing the opposite of what he says. When he yells "Move!" she stares past him, just wagging her tail like she's enjoying herself at the beach. Or if he screams, "Stay!" she suddenly has the urge to slowly mosey somewhere else with that dull, blank, drooping jowls, old-dog-look . . . "Yeah, right kid."

But my son is pretty smart. Now when he has his battles with the dog and she doesn't listen, he turns his attention to me, "Dad, tell her to stop." I can say the exact same thing as my son, and even say it with half as less force, and Lois instantly does what I say. Why? Because Lois is my dog. I had Lois trained before my son was even born. I'm her master.

We have an adversary too. The Bible says that our adversary is the devil (1 Peter 5:8, Ephesians 6:12). And no matter how loud we yell in our own authority, the devil doesn't have to listen to us because we are not his master. But he does have to listen to his real Master. When God speaks, Satan must listen. And so the proper way to overcome the devil is not to shout at him but to first submit and appeal to the Master (James 4:7). Only in the authority of Jesus do we have victory over the evil one. Only when we are connected to God and have his support will we be able to outwit and outmatch the enemy.

Our adversary is after our heart. The way the devil seeks to destroy us is to get us to lose faith. And the way we lose faith is by taking our eyes off of God and onto the world. Remember, Luke 18:1-8 takes place in the context of Luke 17:22-37. There Jesus explains that we will have to endure times that resemble the days of Noah and Lot, godless times where people reveled in sin.

In Luke 17:32, Jesus says, "Remember Lot's wife." That's it. That's the whole verse. It's a bit curious of Jesus to say that and not elaborate. But when you do what he says and remember what happened to Lot's wife, it makes a lot of sense.

Lot's wife looked back at Sodom and Gomorrah and instantly turned into a pillar of salt (Genesis 19:26). Like Lot's wife who couldn't resist looking back at the life she was leaving, we will lose our heart if we stop praying so we can look back at the godless world we are leaving as we journey forward with Christ. She took her eyes off God's promises and future for her and clung to her past, and it was her undoing.

The point Jesus made in Luke 17:32 when he said "Remember Lot's wife" comes full circle in Luke 18:8 where he states, "I tell you, he will give justice to them speedily. Nevertheless, when the Son of Man comes, will he find faith on earth?" Lot's wife clung to her old life because she could not embrace the promises of a future life (Luke 17:33). God told her plainly what was going to happen in the future so she could act rightly through the trials in her present. But she didn't believe God, and so her behavior suffered.

Jesus tells us the future so we will put our faith in him during the present. He tells us what's going to happen so we will believe God, which will cause our behavior to be righteous.

Satan seeks to hinder our prayer life because praying is all about keeping our eyes on God. When we take our eyes off of God and stop believing the truth about him, that's when our behavior begins to falter.

Behavior follows beliefs. What you believe about God will manifest in what you do and how often you pray.

Pray Always Because God Wins

In Luke 18:8 Jesus is referring to his second coming. He is seeking to motivate us to pray and not lose heart by telling us how the larger story is going to end.

By pointing to his second coming he's spurring us on by saying, "Hey guys, I know things are going to get pretty bleak here on earth. You're going to be persecuted, you're going to feel unloved at times, and you're going to lose some people that you really care about. You may not get the job you want or the marriage you thought you would have. Your church might split. You may have many unmet dreams here on earth. But remember, in the end of the story, God wins."

Jesus knows that the only reason we will stop praying and give up is if we start to believe there is no hope, if we start to believe that the story does not end well for the Kingdom of God. But we should always have hope no matter how bleak it looks because in God's sovereignty he has already written the end of the story. It's not going to be a nail-biter. When Jesus comes back to earth in glory and splendor and in all of his holy majestic strength, no one is going to wonder if he is the winner. Everyone is going to fall on their knees at the sight of his return and know he is the victor. Jesus points out the end of the story in Luke 18:8 so we will have the motivation to not lose heart in the middle of the story in which we are currently living.

Again, Luke 18:8 states, "I tell you, he will give justice to them speedily. Nevertheless, when the Son of Man comes, will he find faith on earth?" I think it would be fair to interpret this verse by saying it this way as well, "However, when the son of man comes, will he find people [praying] on the earth?" For to have faith is to express it in prayer. A lack of faith will always correspond with a lack of prayer. An abundance of faith will always correspond with an abundance of prayer. Faith and prayer are like inhaling and exhaling, you can't have one without the other. When one stops the other stops too and the person dies.

Faith is the fuel in the furnace of prayer. The more fuel you have, the hotter the furnace burns. The more faith you have, the hotter your prayers will burn. What is faith? "Now faith is the assurance of things hoped for, the conviction of things not seen" (Hebrews 11:1). In one sense, faith is an active trust in the future promises God has already accomplished but that we have not yet fully seen.

If we need faith to pray, and faith is tied to our belief in the future, is it any wonder why Jesus has told us the future in Luke 18:8 if his intention is to help us always pray and not give up (Luke 18:1)?

A Right Perspective of the Future Creates Prayers of Faith

At a different time Jesus predicted the future in Matthew 24:11-13 and said, "And many false prophets will arise and lead many astray. And because lawlessness will be increased, the love of many will grow cold. But the one who endures to the end will be saved."

False prophets will hurt the people because they will teach them false things about God. When we believe false things about God, our behavior will be negatively affected too, which is why lawlessness will increase the more we believe false teachers. Our "love will grow cold" for God when we believe false doctrines because what we believe about God always affects our behavior.

Throughout Luke 18:1-8, Jesus teaches us that the way to endure to the end will be by resisting our adversaries in prayer, keeping our eyes fixed on Jesus, and then we will not lose heart and we will endure to the end. As we've already stated, the last way Jesus helps us to always pray so we don't lose heart is by reminding us that God has already written the future and won.

Notice the connection between our prayers and our beliefs about the future found in 1 Peter 4:7, "The end of all things is at hand; therefore be self-controlled and sober-minded for the sake of your prayers." Our belief about how the story will end has a direct impact on our prayer life.

I find it interesting that when Peter tells us how to overcome our adversary, he uses similar language as he did in 1 Peter 4:7. In 1 Peter 5:8 he states, "Be sober-minded; be watchful. Your adversary the devil prowls around like a roaring lion, seeking someone to devour." In 1 Peter 5:8 we are to be "sober-minded" so we can overcome the devil. In 1 Peter 4:7 we are told to be "sober-minded for the sake of your prayers." Keeping a right perspective on how this story is going to end will help us be sober-minded, being sober-minded helps us to pray, and prayer is directly related to our effectiveness in resisting our adversary.

In Ephesians 6:12 we are told that we wrestle "against the spiritual forces of evil in the heavenly places." We are then told to put on the full armor of God in Ephesians 6:13-17. But then we are quickly told in Ephesians 6:18 that while we should put on the full armor of God we must also be "praying at all times in the Spirit, with all prayer and supplication. To that end keep alert with all perseverance . . . ." Prayer is essential to persevering over the lies of Satan.

Prayer is so powerful in our defense and offense against Satan because keeping our eyes firmly fixed on Jesus is key to persevering faith, "And let us run with perseverance the race marked out for us, fixing our

eyes on Jesus, the pioneer and perfecter of faith"
(Hebrews 12:1-2, NIV). Satan wants us to look at
anything other than Christ so we will lose heart and
give up. God tells us to always pray so we will always be
looking to Jesus, to the truth. In the ESV, Hebrews 12:2
is stated this way, "looking to Jesus, the founder and
perfecter of our faith." If we want faith, we need to
look to Jesus, for he perfects "our faith."

God has promised us victory in Christ. And In Luke 18:8,
Jesus reminds us of the promised future so we will live
well in the present.

Powerful Prayers Happen When We Pray in Alignment with God's Promises

Jesus tells us to look ahead to his second coming so we
will not be distracted with the trials that we will go
through before he comes.

Knowing the future isn't just meant to be something
cool and fun. Knowing what God has promised is meant
to be a guide in our prayer life. When you align your
prayers with the promises God has already made, you
are praying the most powerful prayers possible.

Certainly God really does change things when we pray
about them. Some people really do pray more effective
prayers than other people (James 5:16-18). So none of
what we are saying here means God only answers
prayers that he was going to answer anyways, thus

making the act of prayer a formal, symbolic, and useless endeavor.

How prayer works in correlation to God's predetermined will is mysterious, but not contradictory. When God does things we don't understand, like using free human's prayers to accomplish his fixed will, it is simply more evidence that he really is God and we are not, for his thoughts and ways really are higher than ours (Isaiah 55:8-9). It points to his glory when he does things we can't comprehend. And just because we can't comprehend it doesn't mean it's not logical, believable, biblical, and true.

But although God accomplishes his will through the prayers of his saints, he never contradicts his will because of the saints. Therefore, it's safe to state this biblical principle: Aligning your prayers with the will of God makes your prayers more powerful.

That's why it is so crucial to know what the will of God is. When God gives us promises, he gives us the opportunity to pray powerful prayers that will be answered. The widow in Luke 18 made her request to the judge because it was supposed to be his desire to give justice. She was asking for something that should have been the judge's will.

Likewise, our requests to the Judge are always more powerful when our prayers correspond to the desires God already has. 1 John 5:14-15 explains, "And this is the confidence that we have toward him, that if we ask anything according to his will he hears us. And if we know that he hears us in whatever we ask, we know that we have the requests that we have asked of him."

Jesus said in Luke 18:7-8, "And will not God give justice to his elect, who cry to him day and night? Will he delay long over them? I tell you, he will give justice to them speedily. Nevertheless, when the Son of Man comes, will he find faith on earth?" That's a promise! "I tell you, he will give justice to them speedily." But Jesus then asks the question, "Nevertheless, when the Son of Man comes, will he find faith on earth?" It's as if Jesus is saying, "I just told you the future. I just told you what to pray. I just told you why you should pray. But will you pray?"

As we come to a close, after all this studying about the sovereignty of God, Jesus leaves us with a question, leaving room for no doubt that our prayer life is going to be lame or passionate, weak or powerful, because of the choices we as individuals make.

And the choice we are encouraged to make throughout Luke 18:1-8 is not to be persistent, but faithful.

Powerful and Passionate Prayers Are Not the Result of Persistence but of Faith

After reading how this widow would not stop asking the judge for what she wanted, the temptation is to assume that we should never stop asking God for what we specifically want. But this passage of Scripture is not showing us that we ought to always pray about one thing until we get it.

As Jesus made clear, as soon as we pray, God hears us and will answer us. The manifestation of the answer make take a minute, a year, or only be revealed in heaven, but God answers quickly. It's not wrong to keep praying about one thing if we feel led by the Holy Spirit to do so, but we must make sure we are not under the assumption that God only hears our prayers *because* of our persistence, "And when you pray, do not heap up empty phrases as the Gentiles do, for they think that they will be heard for their many words. Do not be like them, for your Father knows what you need before you ask him" (Matthew 6:7-8).

The danger in endlessly requesting the same thing over and over again until you get it is that eventually your prayers become "empty phrases" and not a conversation. Asking your Father for what you desire is very different than badgering him with your wish list.

I believe God sometimes holds back giving us what we ask for because he knows it will harm us, for God only gives his children "good gifts" (Matthew 7:11). But because we keep asking and talking about nothing else, he grants our request to get us unstuck. Of course he knows we will suffer the consequences. God disciplines us by finally giving us what we won't stop asking for because he knows only then will we begin to truly pray again. Sometimes the scariest thing is when God finally says "yes" to when he's been consistently saying "no." Remember what happened when Israel kept asking for a king (1 Samuel 8:10-22) or when they really wanted meat to eat in the desert (Numbers 11:18-20)?

Perhaps Luke 18:1-8 is sending us the opposite message of praying persistently to get what you want. Perhaps Jesus is saying that, yes, pray always. But don't endlessly pray about one thing as though God is an unjust judge who needs your persistence to do what's best for you. I think it's worth mentioning that the phrase "persistent widow" doesn't actually show up in the text. This is usually a header modern Bible editors have put over this text as a title. When you read the actual passage, it seems to the emphasis is not so much on persistence but on faith, and there is a difference. Persistence is not stopping until you get what you want. Faith is believing God no matter what. Jesus didn't ask, if he will find persistence when he returned; he asked, "Nevertheless, when the Son of Man comes, will he find *faith* on earth?" (Luke 18:8).

I have recently been praying a lot about one request. It was good for awhile to spill my heart out to God, to be brutally honest about some dreams I hope will one day come true. But after a period of time, I could tell the intentions of my prayers were beginning to shift. My persistence in prayer was beginning to be an expression of my lack of faith. I could feel that I was bombarding God with the hope of getting him to answer this specific request now. It was as though I felt God was looking for me to pray super hard and only then would I receive the request.

This type of prayer motivation is unbiblical. No prayer is answered for any other reason other than grace. God loves us to pray passionately, but passion is not a prerequisite for power. God supplies power when he wants. After awhile, I felt the Lord saying something like, "I've heard your prayers, son. I've heard you, Mark. That's enough, let's move forward now. Leave it in my hands. I love you. I'll do what's best."

Certainly we should keep doing the practical things necessary in our own power to allow God to bless us the way we desire (Example: If you are praying to be a doctor, you still need to go to medical school). But eventually our persistence over one certain prayer can be an expression of a lack of faith rather than an expression of faith.

Faith in God Results in Passionate and Powerful Prayers

When Jesus closed with the question, "Nevertheless, when the Son of Man comes, will he find faith on earth?" (Luke 18:8), what is he hoping we will be putting our faith in? Faith in what? In the truth about God of course.

If we have faith in God's goodness, faith that he wants to have a conversation with us, faith that he is powerful enough to do whatever he wants, and faith that God has already won in the future, then our prayer life will never be the same.

Luke 18:1 says that Jesus told this parable because we "ought always to pray and not lose heart." Jesus asked in Luke 18:8, "Nevertheless, when the Son of Man comes, will he find faith on earth?" The way to always pray and not lose heart is to deeply believe the best of God.

Jesus left us with a real question. He didn't answer it for us. I desperately want to answer his call as I'm sure you do too. Like you, I don't want to lose heart. We all want to love God and people with passion and power.

If we hope to never quit, we must believe God like never before.

Questions:

1. Read James 4:6-7. What are two things Christians should do in our fight against the devil?

2. As we discussed earlier in this study, Luke 17:20-37 sets the context for Luke 18:1-8. Read Luke 17:31-32 and Luke 18:8. What does Lot's wife teach us about faith?

3. How does knowing the future help you live with faith in the present?

4. God has already won the war but the battles still rage on. Do you agree or disagree? Explain.

5. What's the relationship between faith and prayer? If you have a lot of faith in God, how will this manifest in your prayer life? If you have little faith in God, how will this affect your prayer life?

6. Read Jesus' words in Matthew 24:11-13. How does false teaching affect our love for God and people? In other words, how does a lack of faith in the truth affect our love? (Read Galatians 5:6 and James 2:14-26 for assistance.)

7. Read 1 Peter 4:7 and Matthew 25:1-13. How should an awareness of the end drawing near affect the way we live our lives with the time we have left?

8. Read Hebrews 12:1-3. How does keeping your eyes fixed on Jesus affect your faith? Explain.

9. Read 1 John 5:14-15. How does knowing the promises of God and future God has promised allow us to pray in alignment with God's will? In other words, how does praying the word of God empower your prayer life?

10. Do you believe Luke 18:1-8 is more about persistence or faithfulness? Explain.

Dear Reader,

Thank you so much for allowing me to take this journey with you through Luke 18:1-8. God taught me so much in this study, and I pray it benefited you just as much as it has me.

If you enjoyed this small group Bible study, would you please do me a giant favor? Would you leave a positive review on Amazon? I'm not asking for my ego! I only ask because the more positive reviews received on Amazon, the more Amazon will naturally promote this study to other people. I want as many people as possible to learn how to pray with passion and power for the glory of God.

Also, please feel free to check out my other books and Bible studies. You can head to Amazon or my online ministry, ApplyGodsWord.com, for more information about my other resources.

Lastly, I would love to give you some free eBooks, blogs, and videos. Just visit ApplyGodsWord.com and let's keep growing together. AGW Ministries is also on YouTube, Twitter, and Facebook. Just head to those platforms and search, "ApplyGodsWord.com" and you should find our home pages. For questions or speaking requests, you can email me at markballenger@applyGodsWord.com.

Thanks again for making me a part of your Bible study!

God bless,
-Mark

Made in the USA
Las Vegas, NV
23 December 2022

64074976R00051